MANX CATS

Big Buddy Books
An Imprint of Abdo Publishing
abdopublishing.com

BIG BUDDY CATS

KATIE LAJINESS

abdopublishing.com

Published by Abdo Publishing, a division of ABDO, PO Box 398166, Minneapolis, Minnesota 55439.

Printed in China.
092017
012018

Cover Photo: Alamy Stock Photo.
Interior Photos: ASSOCIATED PRESS (p. 11); Christina Gandolfo/Alamy Stock Photo (p. 25); David Chapman/Alamy Stock Photo (p. 5); Getty Images (pp. 7, 13, 15, 17, 21, 23, 27, 29); Idamini/Alamy Stock Photo (p. 19); Werner Sigg/Shutterstock (p. 9).

Coordinating Series Editor: Tamara L. Britton
Contributing Editor: Jill Roesler
Graphic Design: Jenny Christensen

Publisher's Cataloging-in-Publication Data

Names: Lajiness, Katie, author.
Title: Manx cats / by Katie Lajiness.
Description: Minneapolis, Minnesota : Abdo Publishing, 2018. | Series: Big buddy cats | Includes online resources and index.
Identifiers: LCCN 2017943922 | ISBN 9781532112003 (lib.bdg.) | ISBN 9781614799078 (ebook)
Subjects: LCSH: Manx cat--Juvenile literature. | Cats--Juvenile literature.
Classification: DDC 636.822--dc23
LC record available at https://lccn.loc.gov/2017943922

CONTENTS

A POPULAR BREED

Cats are popular pets. About 35 percent of US households have a cat. And, Americans own more than 85 million!

Around the world, there are more than 40 **domestic cat breeds**. One of these is the Manx cat. Let's learn why the Manx is one of the most popular cat breeds in the United States.

Manx cats came from an island off the coast of England. It is called the Isle of Man. The Manx breed has lived there for hundreds of years.

THE CAT FAMILY

All cats belong to the **Felidae** family. There are 37 **species** in this family. **Domestic cats** are part of one species. Lions and other types of cats make up the others.

Did you know?

Humans and cats have lived together for at least 3,500 years.

Domestic cats and tigers share nearly 96 percent of the same genes. So, they have many of the same features.

MANX CATS

Manx cats date back to the 1750s. They arrived on the Isle of Man with sailors on trading ships. These cats caught rats and mice on board. Without the Manx, **rodents** would have eaten food and spread illness.

Did you know?

King Edward VII was the king of England from 1901 to 1910. He owned Manx cats.

Cats use their whiskers to hunt in the dark. The whiskers feel light movements as other animals move nearby.

Over time, the Manx went from a working cat to a show cat. The Manx **breed** appeared in one of the first American cat shows.

The **Cat Fanciers' Association** was founded in 1906. And the Manx breed was added to the **registry** shortly after. Today, only Manx without tails can appear in shows.

A Manx named Graffiti appeared at the 2015 International Cat Show in Portland, Oregon.

WHAT THEY'RE LIKE

Manx cats are friendly, sweet, and loyal to their owners. And, they get along well with children and other pets.

These felines made excellent working cats in the past. Today, they are still smart and lively. This is what makes them very clever hunters.

Some people think of the Manx as watch cats. They will protect their families and growl at anything they find concerning.

COAT AND COLOR

Cats in this **breed** can have different length coats. All have a double coat. Two layers make the fur thick and warm.

The Manx cat can be any color. And, its coat can be any pattern. Some Manx cats are white, black, or brown. Others have patterns, such as **tabby** or **calico**.

Almost all calico cats are female.

SIZE

The Manx is a medium-sized cat. Both males and females weigh eight to 12 pounds (4 to 6 kg).

Unlike most **domestic cats**, the Manx has a short or missing tail. The **breed's** hind legs are longer than its front legs. And its back end is higher than its shoulders. So, the Manx can hop like a rabbit!

Did you know?

Rumpy is a nickname for a tailless Manx cat.

The Manx has large, round eyes. Its ears are set far apart.

FEEDING

Healthy cat food includes beef, chicken, or fish. A good name-brand food will provide the **nutrients** a cat needs.

Cat food can be dry, semimoist, or canned. Food labels will show how much and how often to feed a cat.

Did you know?

Cats should eat both wet and dry food each day. They get much of their daily water from wet food.

Cats don’t like having their water too close to their food. So, place the food and water bowls in separate areas.

CARE

The Manx needs its coat **groomed** about twice a week. Grooming keeps the coat smooth, especially during shedding season.

Cats also need to have their teeth brushed. Some veterinarians suggest brushing a cat's teeth every day.

A cat should have its claws trimmed every ten to 14 days. It should also have its ears checked to avoid germs.

Manx cats need a good veterinarian. The vet can provide health exams and **vaccines**. He or she can also **spay** or **neuter** cats.

Kittens need to see the vet several times during their first few months. Adult cats should visit a vet once a year for a checkup.

Did you know?

Spaying or neutering a cat may help it live longer. These operations may prevent certain illnesses.

Most cats will wake twice a day to eat and play. They spend the rest of the day napping.

Cats have an **instinct** to bury their waste. So, cats should use a **litter box**. Waste should be removed from the box daily.

A cat buries its waste to mark its area. If a cat goes outdoors, it will begin to do the same. A **microchip** can help bring a cat home if it gets lost.

Cats need toys to keep them entertained. Many cats enjoy toy mice, small balls, and feather wands.

KITTENS

A Manx mother is **pregnant** for 63 to 65 days. Then, she gives birth to a **litter** of two to four kittens. For the first two weeks, kittens mostly eat and sleep.

All kittens are born blind and deaf. After two weeks, they can see and hear. At three weeks, the kittens begin taking their first steps.

As kittens grow, they become more independent and explore their surroundings.

THINGS THEY NEED

Between 12 and 16 weeks old, Manx kittens are ready for **adoption**. Kittens like to be active. So, they need daily exercise. A Manx cat will be a loving companion for about 14 years.

Purebred cats, such as the Manx, are rarely found at animal shelters. Instead, owners usually buy them from a breeder.

GLOSSARY

adoption the process of taking responsibility for a pet.

breed a group of animals sharing the same appearance and features. To breed is to produce animals by mating.

calico a blotched or spotted animal.

Cat Fanciers' Association established in 1906, it is the world's largest registry for pedigreed cats.

domestic cats tame cats that make great pets.

Felidae the scientific Latin name for the cat family. Members of this family are called felines. They include domestic cats, lions, tigers, lynx, and cheetahs.

groom to clean and care for.

instinct a way of behaving, thinking, or feeling that is not learned, but natural.

litter all of the kittens born at one time to a mother cat.

litter box a place for house cats to leave their waste.

microchip an electronic circuit placed under an animal's skin. A microchip contains identifying information that can be read by a scanner.

neuter (NOO-tuhr) to remove a male animal's reproductive glands.

nutrient (NOO-tree-uhnt) something found in food that living beings take in to live and grow.

pregnant having one or more babies growing within the body.

registry a place where official records are kept.

rodent any of several related animals that have large front teeth for gnawing. Common rodents include mice, squirrels, and beavers.

spay to remove a female animal's reproductive organs.

species (SPEE-sheez) living things that are very much alike.

tabby a domestic cat with a striped and spotted coat.

vaccine (vak-SEEN) a shot given to prevent illness or disease.

ONLINE RESOURCES

To learn more about Manx cats, visit **abdobooklinks.com**. These links are routinely monitored and updated to provide the most current information available.

INDEX